WRITING TIPS

STEP-BY-STEP

2 Manuscripts in 1 Book, Including: Outlining and Character Development

Sandy Marsh

More by Sandy Marsh

Discover all books from the Writing Best Seller Series by Sandy Marsh at:

bit.ly/sandy-marsh

Book 1: *How to Write a Novel*

Book 2: *Outlining*

Book 3: *Story Structure*

Book 4: *Plotting*

Book 5: *Character Development*

Book 6: *How to Write a Screenplay*

Themed book bundles available at discounted prices:

bit.ly/sandy-marsh

Table of Contents

OUTLINING

STEP-BY-STEP

ESSENTIAL CHAPTER OUTLINE, FICTION AND NONFICTION OUTLINING TRICKS ANY WRITER CAN LEARN

SANDY MARSH

BOOK 1: OUTLINING

STEP-BY-STEP

Essential Chapter Outline, Fiction and Nonfiction Outlining Tricks Any Writer Can Learn

Sandy Marsh

reparation, damages, or monetary loss due to the information herein, either directly or indirectly.

Respective authors own all copyrights not held by the publisher.

The information herein is offered for informational purposes solely, and is universal as so. The presentation of the information is without contract or any type of guarantee assurance.

The trademarks that are used are without any consent, and the publication of the trademark is without permission or backing by the trademark owner. All trademarks and brands within this book are for clarifying purposes only and are the owned by the owners themselves, not affiliated with this document.

Table of Contents

Introduction

Congratulations on purchasing this book and thank you for doing so. The following chapters will teach you all the important things that you need to know about making an outline. Learning to make an effective outline is an invaluable tool as a writer. It can help the writing of your book to flow more smoothly, work out more conveniently and be organized.

Chapter 1 talks about the basics of making an outline. This will give you a good foundation and understanding of what outlining is all about. Chapter 2 discusses how you can make an outline for a fiction book. Chapter 3 teaches how you can make an outline for a non-fiction book. Chapter 4 lays down the best practices that you should observe when making an outline.

Writing a book can be a daunting task. By using an outline, you can make the process of writing a book simpler and easier. The good news is that it is not hard to make an outline as long as you know what you are doing. An outline is an effective tool and is the secret behind an effective book writing. By learning how to make an outline, you are able to cover a significant part of the actual book-making process. Take the outline as a blueprint, the guide, or architecture, of your book.

Chapter 1: The Basics of Making an Outline

What is an outline?

An outline works as a guide when it comes to writing your book. Take note that a book is a big world. Without a good outline, you can easily get lost in the process of writing your book. An outline ensures that you stay within the plot that you want for your book and that every scene works towards building your story.

It is worth noting that an outline only serves as a guide. A writer has the option whether or not to stick to their outline. Still, having an outline is helpful because it will give you a sense of direction. It is also a useful tool to use to ensure proper sequencing of events or scenes in your book.

There are different ways to make an outline. This book will teach you notable and effective methods to outline a book, both for a fiction book and a non-fiction book. Indeed, learning how to make an outline is an invaluable tool that should be in the arsenal of every writer.

It can be said that an outline is the book itself but in a very simplified version. It can also deal with the technical aspects of the book, such as the timing as to when and how a certain characters or ideas will be presented. Consider the outline as the blueprint or the foundational architecture of your book.

Who uses an outline?

Almost all professional writers use an outline. Some go as far as saying that all writers *should* use an outline. The use of an outline does not just refer to books, but even in other forms of writing. In fact, it is not uncommon even for article writers to write an outline for their more complicated articles. An outline ensures that the focus of your writing and the proper flow remain concentrated. So, if making an outline is really this important, are there known authors who apply them? The answer is yes. Here are some examples to name a few: The author of *Harry Potter*, JK Rowling, James Salter, Paulo Coelho, Sylvia Plath, Jennifer

Egan, William Faulkner, and many other popular writers have admitted the use of outlines in the creation of their works. As you can see, using an outline is considered such an essential skill and tool of a writer that even well-known authors use it regularly.

Should you use an outline? Well, just because you are a writer does not necessarily mean that you are required to make an outline before writing your book. So, whether you want to use an outline or not is a matter of personal preference. Still, it is worth noting that many writers have realized the benefits of using an outline.

The importance of using an outline

It is worth noting that there are some authors who do not use an outline when they write a book. Instead, they simply allow the natural current of the work to drive them to somewhere, hoping that it would be worth telling. However, the truth is that many of these of authors have outlined the book in their mind, so somehow, they still have that sense of direction. Of course, there are also those writers who completely have no idea of what they are writing and just see where the writing goes. After all, when it comes to writing, especially when it comes to writing fiction, there are no hard and fast rules to limit a writer. You are free to write your book in whatever way you want just as you are also free not to write a book. However, if you want to be sure of your sense of direction and not waste your time writing on so many pages only to realize that they do not make sense, then you should use an outline. An outline is also easy to make, yet it will assure you that your book has a good flow and direction.

Now, there are those who say that using an outline will only limit your imagination, so they do not want to use an outline when they write a book. They do not want the outline to "cage" the expression and flow of their ideas. However, this is not the correct way to view an outline. Take note that as a writer, an outline is still just an outline. You are not in any way compelled to follow your outline all of the time. For example, let us say while you are writing the setting of the story as stated in your outline you realize that a different place would be more suitable, then you are free to use that place instead of what is in your outline. Of course, the same principle applies to the other parts of the book.

Again, an outline is a helpful guide that will ensure to give you a sense of direction; it should not, in any way, be seen as an obstacle or a cage that limits your imagination. You are strongly encouraged to stretch and explore the beauty of your mind. In fact, even an outline comes from the creative mind of a writer. The outline can be thought of as the skeleton of the book that you hang the actual story on.

Outlining for fiction vs. Non-fiction

Outlining works for any kind of book, whether fiction or non-fiction. However, making an outline for a fiction book is not the same when you make an outline for a nonfiction book and vice versa. This is because of the inherent differences between the two genres. In a fiction book, for example, a novel, you will need to spend more time outlining the plot of the story and the sequencing of the events.

You should be able to present your characters effectively and build up the story. In the case of a non-fiction book, there is usually no need to build up any story. Instead, you should focus on presenting the right information. Of course, the proper sequence should also be observed. In a fiction book, the outline will be mostly composed of the setting, the characters, and the different events that take place in the story. In a non-fiction book, the outline will be divided into main topics and subtopics regarding technical subjects.

Although there are differences between making an outline for fiction and nonfiction, the use and purpose of an outline still remain the same, and that is to make writing the book easier and more organized.

Plot outline vs. synopsis

Many people use these two terms interchangeably. However, it is worth noting that they are not the same. Take note that when you create a plot outline before even start writing a book you then use the outline as your guide as you write, so that you will be guided on how the story should flow. Writers who use plot outlines are usually called "plotters" since they plot the whole story before they even write it down. This is a good way to avoid writing too many drafts with rejected scenes and pages.

A synopsis is usually written after the completion of the book. It refers to the summary of your story or novel. The synopsis is usually a part of a proposal letter that a writer sends to a potential publisher.

A synopsis can be as short as a single page or even up to five pages. A plot outline can also take a single page but can be longer than five pages. It depends on how much you work on your outline. If you add in more details, then it will be able to guide you once you proceed to write your story. In addition to the story, a plot outline can include a detailed character story and other events.

Some writers already know their story before they even write it. So, if you can come up with the synopsis first, then you can use that as a guide to make a more detailed outline.

Understand the plot of a story

If you are into fiction writing, then it is important for you to know the plot of a story. What is a plot? It is what draws readers into the story. It refers to the arrangement of the story elements. There are generally five parts of a plot: the beginning or exposition, rising action, climax, falling action, and denouement or ending. Let us take a look at them one by one.

Exposition

The exposition is the beginning of a story. Hence, this is the part where you present your characters. Take note that the characters are not the only ones that develop your story. You also need to pay attention to the place, as well as the time. Unfortunately, some people forget about the element of time. Do not forget that Paris today was much different a hundred years ago. It is also important to keep the exposition as interesting as possible. You need to make it grab the interest of your readers; otherwise, they might stop reading your book before they even find out the about good and exciting parts.

Rising action

This is where you build up your story. This is usually where a problem is presented, and the characters take steps to face or solve the problem. This is also what prepares the most exciting part of the story, the climax. The rising action is where you build up the anxiety and the expectations. This is also the part where you start to tug at the hearts and emotions of your readers. The more attached the readers are to the characters, the more powerful the climax and the overall story will be. It is important that a writer build up the story effectively; otherwise, the story may become boring to the reader.

Climax

This is known as the turning point and the most exciting part of the story. This is where the emotions are at their peak. Nothing is ever the same as this point. This is where real and solid changes take place. Usually, immediately right after the climax, everything takes a downhill, relaxes, and prepares for the ending.

Falling action

This is the part where the story falls and takes a downhill, which leads to the ending of the story. Here, the story usually comes together, and the missing pieces are finally resolved. This is also where you reward your audience. Take note that your readers normally associate themselves with the protagonist in the story, so you use this part show them how the protagonist is rewarded for all of his or her labor. This is also a good part to impress on the readers the moral of your story if any.

Denouement

This is the ending of the story. Here, the loose ends are tied, and the questions are finally answered. Of course, it can be a happy ending or a sad ending. A story can even have an open ending where there is technically no end and you leave to the reader the final conclusion of the story.

Why is it important to understand the plot?

As a writer, it is important for you to understand the plot. When you make an outline, you actually work on the plot of your story, such as how are you going to begin the story, how do you present your characters, the time and place, etc. before then you moving on to the rising action, then the climax, and so on. As you can see, it is important to have a good understanding of the plot because the story revolves around the plot that you set. There are also writers who make an outline by simply filling in the parts of the plot with details.

Chapter 2: Fiction Outline

Snowball Method

The snowball method is one of the most popular techniques for making an outline. Just like a rolling snowball that gets bigger and bigger as it rolls downhill, the snowball method starts with just a simple topic, idea, or a scene. It will then be continuously developed, and it will branch out to more ideas, more scenes, and other parts of the story.

For example, let's start with the simple idea of a man who falls in love with a woman. Let this idea be the very center of the snowball. This will also be the main theme of the story. We now branch out a little and give them each a name. Let us say that the name of the man is Jack and the name of the woman is Mina. So now we have the protagonists of the story, as well as the central theme of love. Of course, Jack cannot just fall in love with Mina out of nowhere. So, we add another part to our snowball: let us say for example that Mina is in need of money. She then applies for a job at a nearby restaurant which happens to be owned by Jack. Let us say that Mina is able to get the job as a waitress, and she then works as a waitress gets to meet other people who work at the restaurant. Again, this is another part of the snowball.

When working as a waitress, one day, Mina encounters a very rude customer. Again, we let the snowball turn, and we simply continue to add more information or details. For example, let us say that the rude customer is the one who complains and calls for the manager of the restaurant who happens to be Jack as well, the owner. Jack then is able to put the situation under control. That evening, Jack calls Mina to his office for a meeting. Mina is anxious about it because she does not want to lose her job. Again, we simply let the snowball turn and gather more details. Contrary to what she has expected, once she is already in the office, Jack appears to be very polite and even apologizes for what happened that day.

This is simply how the snowball method works. Simply put, you just have to keep adding more and more details. If you continue to do this, then you will soon come up with a short story, a novelette, or even a novel. From one small snowball, you simply let it roll and roll and gather more ideas and details to turn it into a big snowball, a complete story. Also, do not forget that you are writing an outline and not a story just yet. So, keep it simple and short, but be sure that the main points of the story are there.

Pure summary

As the name implies, a pure summary outline is the kind of outline that is composed of summaries. This is like the short version of your entire book or novel. You simply have to summarize everything, such as chapters, scenes, and others.

The idea behind this method is to write down your whole story from beginning to end, but only write down a compressed version. To do this, just write down the important parts or highlights. You can skip all forms of dialogues and just focus on telling what is happening in the story.

For example, Ana is looking for a job and applies as a journalist. She gets the job and as she works as a journalist, she gets to meet Ryan, a photographer, who happens to work in the same company. Despite their busy schedule, they do their best to make time for each other. One day, Ana is in an accident and

Ryan does his best to serve her. To save her life, he has to go into an ancient forest and get a golden apple from a mysterious tree. He ventures into the forest and meets Galdorf, a friendly elf. Galdorf helps him find the mysterious tree and battle the Dark Witch of the forest. By doing so, he frees the imprisoned elves and also saves Ana from dying. They live happily ever after.

As you can see, every part of the story is compressed but it is complete. All that you need to do is to fill in the details. The good thing here is that you are already given a clear roadmap or guideline as to how your story will flow from start to finish. In fact, by using this approach, you will already be able to imagine your story as a whole, and all that you need to do is to write down the details to make the story come alive.

The pure summary is one of the best ways to make an outline. Just summarize every chapter or sub-chapter from beginning to end. When done, you will have a complete story. All that you need to do is to clarify every point by adding in more details.

Skeletal outline

You have probably learned this kind of outline in school or for any other academic purposes. The key to this method is to input the core points in the right order that will best present your story. This is an effective way to get a bird's eye view of your story, including its overall structure. Take note that the structure of a book or story is essential. A book that is poorly structured, whether fiction or non-fiction, will most probably have problems with being disorganized and have confusing contents. A skeletal outline will allow you to easily reform your story or book, which will allow you to create the maximum impact out of your story. Let us take a look at a simple example of a skeletal outline:

Exposition

- The setting of the story takes place in a small village called as Sestin.

- The story introduces Adam, who is a farmer.

- The story then introduces Monica, the daughter of a rich businessman

Rising action

- Adam meets Monica as he tends the farm of her father.

- They get to know each other for some days.

- One day, goblins attack the village of Sestin.

- Monica is held hostage by the goblins.

Climax

- Adam fights the goblins and saves Monica.

- The story also reveals that they both share the same mutual feeling for each other.

- It is found that Adam is actually of royal blood and owns a kingdom

Falling action

- The father of Monica allows Adam to marry his daughter

Denouement

- Adam and Monica get married and everyone is happy.

- They all live happily ever after.

Take note that this is just an example of a skeletal outline. It may be shorter or even much longer than this. The important thing is to plot the story and the events properly. It is also worth noting that this kind of outline is not just applicable to fiction writing. You can also use it for non-fiction works. This will be discussed in more detail later in the book.

A good thing about this approach is that it allows you to see the structure of your book more clearly. Usually, a skeletal outline clearly divides the book into parts and is just composed of single lines. When taken together, they all compose a whole story.

Bullet outline

- A bullet outline is one of the most common types of outlining. In fact, this is one that is widely used by people even if they do not read about it. With a bullet outline, you simply have to make notes in bullet form as to what will happen in the story. For example:

- Lisa is an accountant.

- One day, she meets Mr. Gibson, a high-stakes gambler.

- They get to know each other better.

- They fall in love with each other.

- However, Mr. Gibson's gambling addiction starts to become a problem and begins to affect their relationship.

- Lisa tries to help Mr. Gibson and does her best to save their relationship.

- (and so on and so forth)

This is an example of a bullet outline. So, how do you use this outline? It is actually fairly simple. Using the example, at first you expound on the part of the outline that says, "Lisa is an accountant." A good way to do this when you actually write your novel is to describe the nature of Lisa's work. Make it as meaningful and interesting as possible.

If you look at the next part of the sample outline, the next part is "One day, she meets Mr. Gibson, a high-stakes gambler." Of course, you would not have to write this line as is. Rather, just like the first bullet, you make it more details. How did they meet? Perhaps Mr. Gibson starts to have money problems and needs an accountant to save his business. You can explore and expound on this once you actually start to write the book. Take note that this single bullet alone can take a whole chapter. This is just to give you an example of how to use a bullet outline more effectively.

A bullet outline is a very simple yet effective method. Another benefit of using this kind of outline is that it gives you a lot of room to exercise your imagination once you start to write the story. The outline focuses more on the flow of the story instead of what is actually happening in the story.

It is common to use a bullet outline on a per chapter basis. Many writers first prepare an outline in bullet form before they begin writing a chapter. This way, they can be sure that they know the direction of the story. Every bullet point is also usually short, so it would not be hard for you to follow it. Once you have a well-established outline in bullet form, then all you need to do is fill in the details of every bullet point and not worry about the direction that your story will take.

Chapter outline

A chapter outline divides a story into chapters. Every chapter will then have an outline of what is going to happen in that particular chapter. Here is an example:

Chapter 1: The Meeting

Noah calls for all the soldiers to attend the secret meeting.

Every soldier attends the meeting, except for Jason.

Jason, the number one soldier in the world, wakes up in a hospital with amnesia.

Even though Jason is not able to attend the meeting set by Noah, Noah is soon able to follow his tracks and visits him in the hospital.

Noah reminds Jason who he really is.

As you can see from the example, the book will be divided into chapters and every chapter will then be divided into subtopics or events that take place in the story. A chapter outline is a good method, especially if you are particular with every chapter in your book.

As is usual, only the main points are included. This is to give room for you to exercise your creative imagination when you write the story. The outline is just enough to guide you as to what will happen next and avoid the situation where you get stuck up not knowing how to make the story to flow continuously. A chapter outline is also one that is commonly used by writers.

Sequence outline

A sequence outline puts more focus upon the sequencing of the events in the story. However, it still outlines the important points, so even this method alone would be enough to help you with writing your book. Here is an example of this kind of outline:

1 - Dianne, still a very young child, is baptized as a witch.

2 - Her parents were killed for practicing sorcery.

3 - She soon grows into one of the most powerful witches.

4 - Dianne meets King Gregory, the man who had ordered for her parents to be burned at the stake.

(and so on and so forth)

As you can see, there is a fine outline of the sequence of the events. If you are the type of writer who finds it hard to stick to the flow of your story, then a sequence outline may be the one for you.

Although you can add in as many details as you want, it is important to stick to the sequence; otherwise, a change may have major effects on the story as a whole. Take note that if you mess up with even just one part of the sequence, then you should check how it affects the other parts. Are they still logical enough when taken together? This method is also commonly used by writers. It is also like a bullet form outline but is more particular with the sequence of the events and the flow of the story.

Flowchart outline

This approach makes use of a flowchart. This is similar to a sequence outline but makes use of a chart that is also in proper sequence. Here is a simple example:

Adam works as a painter --> He attends an event for artists --> While at the event, he sees and meets Stella --> He falls in love with her at first sight --> and so on and so forth.

As you can see, the scenes or parts of the chapters are reflected through this flowchart. When you finally start working on the book, then you will add in the details to every point in the chart. A single part of the flowchart can cover a few pages up to a whole chapter, depending on what is happening in your story. So, for example, let us take the first part of the flowchart: Adam works as a painter. When you write this in your book, you can then expound on this topic. You describe the nature of his work and you can also write and show what happens in his life as a painter. As you can see, just these things alone can take many pages, even a whole chapter.

The thing with a flowchart method, just like any other outlining method, is for you to pinpoint the main parts of the story and ensure that you arrange things in the right order. Once everything is set, then you simply have to add the details when you write the book.

Visual outline

If you are fond of drawing, then this style of outlining may be the one for you. When you use a visual outline, all that you need to do is to draw the main events in a story, especially its plot. Take note that instead of writing in words, this approach lies in drawing and making figures. For this, you may want to use a notebook. You can fill each page with a drawing that would illustrate what the scene will be. You then follow it up with another scene on the next page, and so on and so forth.

Even if you cannot draw well, you can still use this approach. After all, just like any other outlines, this is something that you do not need to show to anyone else. An advantage of using drawings instead of words in making an outline is that you will have more room to play with the words, as well as for the exercise of your imagination. This is because every drawing can have diverse meanings and significance. If you want a style of outline that will give you maximum use of your imagination once you begin writing your book, then perhaps using a visual outline is a good idea. However, the drawback is that this kind of outlining may not always work for everyone. In fact, the very reason why you want to make an outline is to have a good sense of direction when you finally write your book. The risk is that you may not be so inspired when you finally write your book that the drawings may start to look boring or empty to you.

Chapter 3: Non-Fiction Outline

Pure summary

Just like for fiction writing, you can also use the pure summary approach for non-fiction book writing. When you use this approach, simply make a summary of the information. This means that you do not have to explain anything. Just make a summary of every chapter in the book. For sub-topics, you can simply write a one or two-sentence summary. Again, this is just a summary, so there is no need for you to expound or explain anything. Still, it is worth noting that when you read a summary, the stories must be coherent and logical enough. In other words, it must still be a complete story with proper flow and structure. However, of course, you do not want for it to too detailed. After all, it is just a summary, which can be a summary per chapter or even per sub-topic in every chapter. The important thing is for the summary to mention the main points of the book. This will also ensure that you will not forget about them.

When you use this method, then it is also important that you pay attention to the sequence of the information. A common rule in non-fiction writing is to start from the basics, and then gradually branch out to more complicated matters on the subject.

In non-fiction, you are not expected to make a well-detailed summary considering that there is a chance that you still need to learn more specific details about the topic in question. Of course, if you know exactly what you are writing about then you may only require a minimum level of research; however, if you are writing something about which you do not have enough knowledge, then there would be little that needs to be summarized. If you want, you can just research and study the subject first before you start to make a pure summary outline. However, do not let the lack of research prevent you from using this approach. After all, you have the convenience of having open books and information both when you make an outline and when you write the book.

Skeletal outline

A skeletal outline is common in non-fiction writing, especially when the book deals with a technical topic. This is because a skeletal outline offers exactly what you would need for non-fiction writing. When you use this approach, you begin with a subtitle, which may be the name of your chapter. You then identify and specify the skeletal outline of the book with the topics and sub-topics that you will discuss in the book. Needless to say, this follows the same format as the one for fiction. However, unlike a fiction book, this does not follow any plot. Rather, it has a more logical flow to it. For example, when you write a book about bitcoin, you should not talk about bitcoin mining right away. Instead, you should start with the basics, such as what bitcoin is, what a cryptocurrency is, and others, and then make your way up from there.

Bullet outline

A bullet outline is excellent when you deal with specifics. For example, when you make an outline of a chapter or sub-chapter in a book. Also, what you can do is to highlight the name of a chapter, and then simply outline in bullet form what you want to talk about for that part of the book. For example, let us say that you want to write a book about the cryptocurrency Bitcoin, here is a sample outline:

Chapter 1: The Basics of Bitcoin

- What is Bitcoin?

- What is cryptocurrency?

- What is a cryptocurrency wallet?

- Who uses bitcoin

- How does a bitcoin transaction work?

- (and others)

As you can see, every point is made clear. All that is left for you to do is add the details. Of course, you can further use the bullet outline like this:

Chapter 1: The Basics of Bitcoin

- What is Bitcoin?

  - a digital money

  - uses cryptography

- What is cryptocurrency?

  - cryptography for secure communication and transaction

- What is a cryptocurrency wallet?

  - a place to store cryptocurrency

  - kinds of cryptocurrency wallets (hot and cold wallets)

- Who uses bitcoin

- anyone with an Internet connection

- How does a bitcoin transaction work?

  - Input

  - Recipient's wallet address

  - Amount

As you can see, this makes it more detailed and it will be easier to fill in the information once you start writing the book. When you write non-fiction, outlining your work is more practical. After all, non-fiction works do not deal so much with one's creative imagination. The important thing is for you to be able to cover the technical details and be able to present them effectively.

Chapter outline

A chapter outline is one of the simplest ways to make an outline for a non-fiction book. Basically, you simply have to write the name of the chapter, and then add in the titles of the sub-topics within a chapter. This is also like a bullet form of outlining but is more general. Of course, you can also make it more specific by further outlining the sub-topics just like in a bullet outline. In fact, both kinds of outline are very similar to each other.

The first step in a chapter outline is to set the titles of the chapters. Again, as a rule in non-fiction, you should start with the basics. The reason is that you must first establish a foundation for your readers before you delve into more complicated matters. A common mistake committed by writers is to assume that the reader already knows and understands the topic. If you come to think of it, this understanding is highly flawed. After all, a reader would not have to waste time reading your book if he is already aware or if he already understands what is written in your book. So, never assume that the reader can easily understand what you write. Instead, have an open mind and consider the reader as someone who knows nothing about your subject. Of course, this is subject to some exceptions, for example, if you target readers are really those who already have an idea of your subject. A good example of this will be the advanced guides or manuals.

Once you have the titles of the different chapter ready, then it is time for you to add in the subtitles that will be placed under each corresponding chapter. You should be careful about the subtitles because they are the ones that will lead the development of the book. Hence, they are the ones that will form the structure of the book. Just stick to the basic rule of starting with the basics and then work your way up, and you will be fine. This is just a matter of presentation. Feel free to try different combinations until you find the one that feels most natural and convenient for a reader.

The number of chapters will depend on the kind of book that you write, as well as the number of words of the entire book. Normally, the longer the book is, the more chapters it will include. When you write your outline, be sure to pay attention to how many chapters your book will have, as well as the number of sub-topics that you will be using. It helps if you have more sub-topics so that you will not run out of things to write about. However, take note that book writing is not about the length but the quality if your book. Hence, it is important that you focus more on the quality of your writing that on the number of chapters or subtitles that your book has.

Research

Although not considered as a complete outlining method, when it comes to non-fiction writing, research is the main tool that you have in your arsenal. Although you are still free to use your imagination, non-fiction writing has certain restraints upon one's writing. The golden rule is that you cannot contradict a fact. Well, except, of course, if you have another set of facts to present that can support your view. Take note that when it comes to non-fiction writing, the facts are your friends. Needless to say, in a non-fiction book, almost everything that you write should be backed up by research or at least verifiable. This is to make your writing more believable and credible.

In non-fiction writing, it does not matter how good your outline is if you do not understand the subject. Hence, make sure that you have all the necessary materials to get to know your subject and do as much research as possible. The more that you know your subject, the easier it will be for you to come up with a good outline, and the easier it will be for you to complete the book.

Chapter 4: Best Practices

Know your characters

When you write a story, especially in fiction writing, it is important for you to know your characters. It is worth noting that an outline is not something that you use to get to know your characters. It is important for you to know the characters first before you make an outline.

Take note that the characters are important as they are the ones that tell and develop the story. If there are not enough characters or if you do not know your characters well enough, then the story will not grow properly. Therefore, is important for you to know and understand who your characters are. In fact, once you know your characters, then telling the story will come naturally as the characters themselves will play out the story. This is the part of writing a story where the writer becomes a mere observer of his characters. You can allow your characters to lead you. This will give you an idea of what the story will be and, so it will be easier for you to make an outline.

If you do not know your characters yet, especially your main characters in the story, then you should give yourself more time to get to know them. You do not necessarily have to know all your characters completely. You will know if you already have sufficient understanding of your characters when the characters themselves are able to lead and create the story for you. Needless to say, every character must have his or her own persona and should act according to that personality.

A suggested way to know your characters is to interview them one by one. This is a common practice used by novel writers. So, how does it work? Just imagine talking to your character. Ask them questions and see and feel how they respond. This may seem strange to some people, but many writers use this approach. They talk to their characters to the point like they feel that they are merely recording (writing) what the characters in the story are telling them. Once characters are given a persona and existence in the story, it will seem that they really have an identity and life of their own. Hence, talk with your characters and ask them questions. Learn from them. This way you will be more able to develop your story.

Know your story

Take note that your plot is like the skeleton of your story. Therefore, when you write a plot it is also important that you already have an idea of what your story is going to be. When you write an outline, it is not important for you to know the minor details and the dialogues of the characters. However, it is important for you to know the main points of your story or the main events that will shape your story. These are the things that will constitute your outline.

The more that you know your story, the easier it will be for you to make an outline of it. After all, making an outline is as simple as recording essential details and skipping dialogues and other things that are considered important to a novel. It is more focused on simply having a worthwhile story instead of discussing all the things that happen in a story.

Now, it is also worth noting that many writers write an outline even without knowing their story. How is this possible? Well, they allow the process of outlining to reveal the story to them. To do this, you just need a basic idea. You write it down as part of an outline, and then simply add more details to it to continue to grow your idea. Since you are just making an outline, it does not have to be too detailed, and you should just focus on the main points that will help develop the story.

Keep it simple

It is important to keep your outline simple. Remember that your outline should not be a cage that will limit your imagination. Rather, it should serve as a guide that will help you come up with a meaningful story. Therefore, keep your outline simple, including only the main and important points that should be in your story.

As a rule, small or minor details should not be placed in an outline, except if they are important to the story. The reason why you do not include everything in your outline is to prevent the outline from limiting you to exercise your imagination as you write your story. Again, an outline should only serve as a guide.

You also do not have to make your outline beautifully worded. Do not forget that the outline is only for your own eyes, so you do not have to spend so much effort in finding the right combination of words. You can save such effort for when you finally write the book. Instead of worrying about the words that you use, focus on the story that you want to tell, as well as the flow of the events and information.

Be flexible

It is worth remembering that an outline only functions as a guide. As such, it is not required for you to always stick to your outline. This is important for you to remember, especially if you suddenly come up with a better idea than the one in your outline while writing the story. This is another reason why you should keep your outline as simple as possible. By keeping it simple and just including the important parts of the story, then you will have more room to exercise your imagination.

It is considered very common for writers to suddenly stray away from their original outline. This is why you should not spend so much time worrying about how your outline is written. After all, it is still just a guide for you; and being the writer, you are free not to follow your outline.

Flexibility is important. Normally, the story only reveals itself fully even to the writer only when you actually pen down the story. This may sometimes come as a surprise, even to the author himself. As you write your book, the more you realize what the story is really all about. Simply put, as you follow your outline, you are also led to discover more about it. Now, from time to time, you may have to change course and take a completely different one than what you have originally outlined. This is normal, but just be sure to take a better path than the previous or current one. Also, if you ever change your course, you may want to stop for a while and reflect on the direction of your new outline.

A normal part of flexibility is to be flexible enough to update your outline. Yes, an outline can undergo so many changes and modifications as you write your book. Take note that you do not need to write new outlines, rather you can just edit your current outline little by little.

A common mistake committed by writers is to change a part in an outline and then allow the new storyline to lead the way without him knowing where it will actually go. Then this happens, then it is as good as writing without an outline. Now, I am not saying that this approach is wrong. Again, there are no hard and fast rules about how to write a book. However, if you are the type who cannot write properly and organize your thoughts without a guide, then what you should do in this case is to update your outline. Yes, updating an outline is something that you should do every time you make even minor changes to your outline. The outline must remain logical and coherent all throughout. This will ensure that your novel or the story itself will also be logical, coherent, and well structured. After all, your very story is just the outline itself, only that it now has more details. For example, if your outline says that Samantha is beautiful, then your story will make descriptions or show certain scenes to show just how beautiful she is. Still, the very essence of the writing can be traced back to your simple outline. Outlining and being flexible go hand in hand. Although there are writers who stick completely to their original outline and do not let anything divert their path (which is not wrong per se), sometimes it is good to be more open and allow changes to take place, especially positive changes.

Have a clear premise

Even before you work on an outline, you should first establish your premise. Ask yourself:

- Who is/are my main character/s in the story?

- Where does the story take place? In what year or time?

- What is the conflict in the story?

- What will be the turning point of my story?

- What message do I want the story to communicate to the readers?

- Who will be the enemies in the story, if any?

Once you have answered all these questions, then it means that you have a good idea of what your story will be. Take note that these are just basic questions. You are free to expound and ask more specific questions. But, these questions will reveal to you the premise of your story or what it is really about. Now, in case you find it hard to answer these simple questions, then it only means that you need to think about your story even more. Do not forget that an outline can only be made if you have a story to tell. Although an outline does not need a complete story, it requires that its essential elements should be present.

When you ask yourself these questions, it is important that you be completely honest with yourself. It is unfortunate that some writers delude themselves and hate saying" I don't know." Take note that this is a normal part of the writing process. The more that you admit to yourself the parts in your story that are still unclear to you, then the more you will understand what your story is really about. After all, the act of writing is still an act of self-discovery. You do not need to have the answers right away. It is normal to accept that you do not know the answers to some questions; the important thing is not to stop to seek for an answer. Of course, to do this, you need to reflect and delve more into your story.

Take a break

Just as you take some breaks to finish writing a book, you should also give yourself time to take a break when you are working on an outline. It is not uncommon for professional writers to spends days just to work on their outline. If you are just starting out to learn how to write and use an outline, then feel free to take as much time as you need. Just do not forget that an outline should make the writing of the book to easier in the long run. Unfortunately, some writers get too caught up writing their outlines that they fail to even start writing the actual book.

You will also be able to think much more clearly and be more creative if you allow your mind to relax. In fact, writers are strongly advised to give themselves a break from time to time even while working on the actual book. It is not uncommon to find writers who go to the beach and spend time on vacation while working on a book. This is because you will be a much more effective writer when you allow yourself to rest. With a fresh and rejuvenated mind, you will be able to use your creative talent more effectively.

Choose and organize your ideas

A book comes from an outline. But, where does an outline come from? Yes − an outline comes from ideas. However, it is worth noting that in the process of writing a book, it is very common to experience being bombarded with lots of ideas. For example, let us take a simple example where you present a protagonist in a story. Let us say that your hero is a man who happens to work in secret service for the government. There are tons of different ideas that you can use to show this. There are also many ways by which the story can go. Does he have super powers? Is he going to die and then resurrect? Or is he just an ordinary person who just happens to be good at what he does or maybe he is not even good at his job and merely relies on luck. The thing is that although outlining is a way to record and organize your ideas, you should also choose the ideas that you will be using in your story.

Now, once you have organized the ideas in your mind, it will then be easy for you to plot your story by making an outline. It is simply hard to make an outline when you know that you yourself do not know your story.

Observe proper sequence

When you write your way outline, it is important for you to pay attention to the proper sequence of the events or information. If it is a fiction book, I then the building and arrangement of the story should be in proper order. If you are writing a non-fiction book, then the information should be in an ordered sequence that will make the information more understandable to your audience. This is important especially if you are writing about a technical topic. For a fiction book, you should build up the story from beginning up to the end. In case of a non-fiction book, then you should share the information by starting from the basic details, and then continue building your way up to more complicated topics or sub-topics in the book.

Making an outline is the best way to set the proper sequencing of events of your story. Unfortunately, some writers still write the bulk of words only to end up with a confusing storyline. By making an outline, you can easily work on the sequence of the events of your story. In fact, you will be able to view and imagine your story completely, and all that will be left for you to do is to add in the details.

If you ever find yourself having a hard time putting things in the right sequence of ideas or events, then it is usually a sign that you should pause for a while and try to understand what is really going on in your story. Sometimes the logical sequence itself will be the one to guide you as to what to write next.

Focus on the main points

Making an outline is simply making a list of the important points of the book in proper order. You should focus on the main points. For a fiction book, the main points will be the beginning of the story, the rising action, climax, falling action, and the denouement. In the case of a non-fiction book, the main points, of course, would relate to the important details regarding your subject.

It is worth noting that some minor details may also be considered a necessary element in the development of a story. In this case, you can include the said minor details in your outline.

But, what are the main points? How do you know if a certain detail should be considered a main point and be included in your outline or not? Well, it depends. If the detail or information is something that is important in building up the story, then it is to be considered a main point and should be included in your outline. However, if it is something that your book or story can do without, then it is just a minor detail. The important thing about making an outline is to give you a good sense of direction. It has to function as a logical road map of your thoughts even if you forget about your story. After all, it is not uncommon for writers to think of an exciting plot only to have it slip away before they are able to get it written down completely. Whenever this happens, a possible wonderful story is lost to the world.

It does not have to be perfect

An outline does not need to be perfect. Keep in mind that it is just a guide. Hence, there is no need to follow it to the letter. Even if you come up with what you believe to be a perfect outline, know that it is still just an outline. As such, you should not allow yourself to be limited by it.

It is also worth noting that no matter how perfect you think your outline is, there is still a chance that it may be revised or modified. This is true, especially in the case of novels. It is not uncommon for writers to start at something specific only to be taken by the story somewhere more beautiful than they had imagined before writing the book. Does this mean that writing an outline is not important? Of course not. An outline assures that you maintain sense and direction in your story. However, it is worth noting that it considered common for writers to make changes to their outline several times as they write the book. Now, you should be careful when you do this. As a general rule, you should not change your original outline. You must stick to it. However, as an exception, you may change your outline if you are able to come up with a better version of the story. It has to make the story more exciting or meaningful for the readers. If not, then you need to stick to your outline. This is the reason why you should not aim to have a perfect outline because such a thing simply does not exist.

Although you do not expect an outline to be perfect, it does not mean that the outline can just contain every thought that you think would be good for your story. An outline must still be carefully written. How can you expect for your outline to guide you if the ideas do not match up well with one another or if the outline itself fails to follow a logical sequence? Hence, it is important that you work on your outline, but do not aim for perfection. Having the right ideas and correct flow would be enough.

Now, just because an outline does not have to be perfect does not mean that you should not give it as much time as it deserves. The outline, after all, serves as the foundation of your book. Therefore, take as much time as you need when making your outline, which leads us to the next topic: time.

Remember that an outline is just a guide

Although an outline can be regarded as important, do not forget the fact that an outline is still just your guide. Therefore, you are free to stick to it while you write the book or totally abandon it halfway. However, this does not mean that an outline is no longer important. But, you need to understand this so that you will not end up like other writers who get too obsessed with their outline.

Remember to see and use your outline as a guide in writing the book. You are always free to change or revise your outline as many times as you want and in any way that you deem best.

Take your time

When making an outline, you should take as much time as you need. Although your outline will not be a part of your book, it is still the foundation of your book. Consider it like a business plan or blueprint of your masterpiece.

Although you can make an outline in as fast as a few minutes, it is not uncommon for professional writers to spend even a week to work on an outline. This is true, especially if you want to create a high-quality book.

You should also learn to organize and manage your time. Unfortunately, there are many writers who commit the mistake of procrastinating. The temptation to procrastinate is something that you should watch out for when you write a book. A good way to avoid procrastination is to set daily objectives. For example, aim to be able to finish 15% of your outline every day. Also, take note that writing an outline is just part of the process. The more important part is for you to write your book, which will take more time and effort than writing an outline.

Have your sources ready

This is true, especially if you work on a non-fiction book. You should have your sources ready. This is because sometimes it is hard to look for your sources during the time of actual writing. A good way to keep your outline more organized is to cite your sources in the outline. One of the main reasons for using an outline is to make the work of writing the book easier for you.

You do not have to cite your sources formally. After all, the outline is your own private document. You do not need to show it to your readers or anyone else. The purpose of having your sources ready and to cite your sources is for you to be ready when you write your book. So that when you write the book, you will know exactly where to look for information as you fill in every major and minor topic in your outline. Even fiction writers can use the same approach. After all, many fiction stories also incorporate real-life events. Take, for example, *Da Vinci Code*, which combines fiction with non-fiction information.

When it comes to writing non-fiction, it is important to take note that you should stick to the facts. If you want to force your creative thought and ideas into the page, then you might want to consider shifting to fiction writing. It is worth noting that readers of non-fiction books read not mainly for entertainment or pleasure, but to get as much as useful information as possible. They do not care about your opinions unless your views have a good basis and foundation. Hence, it is important to identify the kind of genre that you want to write in even before you make an outline. This is because the style of writing and even the expectation of the readers have certain distinctions between fiction and non-fiction writing. As for the sources, be sure to quote from credible sources. If possible, use internationally known and accepted formats like APA or Chicago when citing your sources.

Ask yourself questions

Okay, so now you have a clear idea of how to make an outline. But, how do you know which types to include in your outline? The key is to ask yourself questions, the right questions. For example, when writing fiction, let us say that you have a character named Max. Now, ask yourself, who is Max? Let us say that Max is a poet.

Ask yourself who is Max as a poet? What is he like? Once you are able to answer this then you can have something to place in your outline: Max is a poet who writes for a princess who does not even know that he loves her. Next, ask yourself what happens next. You may come up with the next part of the outline, like: A big event is about to take place and Max and the princess are going to attend the said event. The next step is for you to imagine the event and ask yourself what happens to Max at the event, and so on and so forth. As you can see, by simply asking yourself the right questions, you can develop a story.

How about for non-fiction writing? Well, a similar technique can be used. However, if you are dealing with a technical topic, let us say a book about Blockchain technology, then you should ask a different kind of questions. For example: What is blockchain? What are the types of blockchain? What is the history of blockchain? This continues until you come up with a highly informative book.

It is important to ensure that every part of your outline should help develop or enhance the book. This way you can be sure that your book will be interesting and informative.

Okay, so how do you know the right questions to ask? It is simple. You just have to take the perspective of a reader who does not know your book or subject. Therefore, if it is fiction writing or when you write a novel, if you have a character in mind named Gabriel, then ask: Who is Gabriel? What does he do? Where does he live? All these questions will soon open up a whole new story that is full of meaning and value. Now, in the case of non-fiction writing, again just consider that a reader is a beginner in the subject that you are discussing. Therefore, you should start with the basic details and lay down a good foundation. After which, you can then talk about more complicated topics within your subject matter.

Practice

When it comes to learning how to outline properly and more effectively, nothing beats practice. So, if you want to learn how to make an outline, then just start practicing it. Make an outline for the next books that you write. No matter how much you read about it, it remains true that the only way for you to appreciate and realize just how beneficial making an outline can be.

Learning how to write a good outline is just like learning to write good books. This means that you simply have to practice it by applying it regularly. If you get good at writing outlines, then the task of writing a book becomes simpler and more manageable.

You do not have to learn the different ways to outline a book. After all, when you make an outline, you only need to use one method. If you want, you can combine two methods at once. There is no strict rule as to when a particular method should be used over another. Therefore, feel free to use the one that you are most comfortable with.

Indeed, there are some writers who do not like the idea of using an outline. It is worth noting that this book does not make it a requirement or an obligation of a writer to use an outline, but merely shares how helpful an outline can be in the process of writing a book. Therefore, if you strongly prefer not to use an outline, then you are free to do so. In the world of book writing, whether or not you use an outline does not matter in the end. What matters is the final product, which is the book itself. There are writers who use an outline and know for sure how useful it is, while there are those who simply allow the story to unfold like a surprise. The only disadvantage of not having an outline is that it is common to follow a story only to meet a dead end or you just realize that the story has become dull and boring.

An outline assures that before you even start working and writing your boo, you are assured of a good sense of direction. All you need to do is write, and even if all that you do is to stick to your outline and not change any parts of the story but merely add in the details pursuant to your outline, then you can be sure that you will end up with a good book, provided that you have prepared a good outline.

Once again, it is up to you as a writer whether or not to use an outline. The best way to find out what works for you would be to give it a try. Write a book without an outline and then write one that has a proper outline, and see which writing experience is better for you. In the end, it is not about whether or not you have used an outline, but how much the book has made your soul grow in the process.

Conclusion

Thanks for making it through to the end of this book. We hope it was informative and able to provide you with all of the tools you need to achieve your goals whatever they may be.

The next step is to apply everything that you have learned and start making an outline of your book. Learning how to make an outline is one of the best things that should be in the arsenal of every writer. It is useful and makes the book writing process easy and manageable.

If you are a beginner, you might encounter some difficulties writing an outline for the first time. The key is to not be too strict about it. It is worth noting that the methods revealed in this book are also just guides. You, as the writer, has all the right to make your own modifications. In fact, you may want to develop your own way of making an outline. The important thing is for you to know and understand how to use it to help you in writing a book. Keep in mind that there is really no right and wrong way of making an outline as long as it is able to help you write your book. After all, the very purpose of an outline is to help a writer and make the process of writing a book simpler, easier, and more organized.

When you write a book, it is not uncommon to suddenly feel so lost. Some writers have a story to tell but do not know how to start or how to maintain a smooth flow of the pages. This is why making an outline is important. There is a big universe out there, and you need to place only the right stuff into your book in proper order. Indeed, the task of a writer is not an easy thing. But, if you learn how to use an outline, then you have an invaluable weapon that you can use to make the writing process so much easier.

Good luck!

CHARACTER DEVELOPMENT

STEP-BY-STEP

ESSENTIAL STORY CHARACTER CREATION, CHARACTER EXPRESSION AND CHARACTER BUILDING TRICKS ANY WRITER CAN LEARN

SANDY MARSH

BOOK 2: CHARACTER DEVELOPMENT

STEP-BY-STEP

Essential Story Character Creation, Character Expression and Character Building Tricks Any Writer Can Learn

Sandy Marsh

reparation, damages, or monetary loss due to the information herein, either directly or indirectly.

Respective authors own all copyrights not held by the publisher.

The information herein is offered for informational purposes solely, and is universal as so. The presentation of the information is without contract or any type of guarantee assurance.

The trademarks that are used are without any consent, and the publication of the trademark is without permission or backing by the trademark owner. All trademarks and brands within this book are for clarifying purposes only and are the owned by the owners themselves, not affiliated with this document.

Table of Contents

Introduction

Thank you and congratulations for purchasing *"Character Development: Step-by-Step | Essential Story Character Creation, Character Expression and Character Building Tricks Any Writer Can Learn"*.

This book will help you with every aspect of character building, from creating the basic structure for your character to designing their personality and even helping develop them alongside the development of your story. Everything you will learn within' this book will ensure that you are equipped with all of the knowledge you need in order to create characters that are compelling and that your readers can fall in love with.

If you have read the previous five books from this series, then you will know just how important your characters are to your story. This guidebook will provide you with all of the knowledge you need in order to help create strong characters that will move your story forward and assist you in building the powerful and important emotional attachment between your reader and your characters.

Each chapter within' this book will provide you with part of the character building process. Within' that part you will be given step-by-step instructions so that you can easily create the best characters possible, knowing that they have been designed with every necessary feature to make them powerful additions and tools for your storytelling process. Without further ado, feel free to dive on into the character building experience. Enjoy!

Chapter 1: The Basics

It is no secret how important characters are to your story. They are the individuals that the story is about. Therefore, they are responsible for the story itself. They help you create the story, move the story forward, and introduce change and other action along the way. Without characters, there would be virtually no way for you to design a story.

Before we explore how you can build your own characters, we are going to explore the basics and important features of characters. This will help you understand more about why characters are so important and why you need them. It will also give you a foundational understanding of each unique style of character and how they can serve your story overall.

Why Characters Are Important

Stories are essentially created through verbal or written recollections of events that took place. In literary work, thoughts, choices, words, consequences, and actions are all important elements that are responsible for contributing to the plot line. Naturally, these qualities must be expressed in some form or manner. Since these are human qualities, it makes sense then that they would be expressed through a human-based character. Alternatively, such as in children's stories, they may be expressed through animal characters that possess these human-like qualities.

Characters are an important tool used by authors and writers to move stories forward. These are the personalities that give them the power to add the element of thought, action, words, choices, and consequences into their book. Without characters, they would essentially be describing a scene whereby nothing would be happening because there would be no one for it to happen to, for, or as a result of.

In order to establish themselves as useful tools that are used to move a plot forward, characters can be broken down into twelve categories. You will learn more about each of these categories in the next section. However, it is important to understand that each of these categories was designed to help create powerful and useable tools that writers can call on to help them progress the story forward.

Types of Characters

When you read a novel, you may be surprised to know that characters go a lot deeper than you think. In the novel, you watch the characters evolve, and new ones come and go along the way, but you may not understand how much actually goes into the development of these characters. When authors want to create a story that has a great deal of depth and can easily be believed as a real-life person, it is important that they understand the different types of characters that exist and how they can serve their story.

Naturally, fiction characters are made up. While they may be completely based on real people or have certain features borrowed from people that the author knows in real life, they are still made up characters. This is how the author is able to use them to build and move the story along because the characters can be used to achieve any outcome the author desires to create.

The following character styles will introduce you to twelve different types of characters that exist within' stories. By understanding each unique type of character, you can see how they can serve your story. Furthermore, you can decide what style each character will be designed in which will make it easier for you to discover the guidelines for creating the said character in the long run.

Major or Central Characters are characters that the story revolves around. These are the primary characters within' the story, and they are crucial to the development of the story itself. These are the characters who are presented with conflicts and who are responsible for executing the resolutions. Almost every part of the entire novel will revolve around these particular characters. They are often the main character, as well as that character's friends and family, or coworkers, or anyone else who will be used as a recurring character within' the story. These are some of the most important characters within' your novel because without them you will not have a story to tell. You want to emphasize your development on these characters to make sure that they are realistic, believable, and relatable to your readers.

Minor Characters are characters that are used to serve the major and central characters. These characters have a powerful role in helping to move the plot forward and often have as much depth as the major characters do. They are only considered minor characters, however, because they don't tend to recur as frequently as the major characters will and they are not a part of the central story. For example, they may be a sister that lives on another continent but comes to visit for a short time or even a few times for the duration of the novel. Alternatively, it may be a few coworkers that recur here and there but are not a part of the central theme or the majority of the major plot points. These are important characters because they help provide realistic depth to the book by broadening the scope of characters without taking complete attention away from the major characters themselves.

Dynamic Characters is a phrase used to represent characters that change over the course of the novel. Virtually anyone who changes his or her personality, belief system, morals or values, or even simply matures over the course of the novel is considered a dynamic character. These characters typically evolve for reasons primarily relating to the central theme of the book, such as the central conflict or a major crisis that they face that ultimately contributes to the books overall theme. Dynamic characters are not necessarily any one group of characters themselves. However, they can be virtually any character within' the book. The majority of the dynamic characters in a novel will typically be the major characters because these are the ones that are directly moving the story forward through change, as you learned about in previous books within' this book series. They may also turn out to be any other character within' the book, however. So long as a character changes in some noticeable way from the beginning to the end of the book they are considered a dynamic character.

Static Characters are the exact opposite of dynamic characters. These ones do not change over the course of the story. Instead, they remain the same. Completely unchanged. Static characters are not suitable to be major characters because they do not help progress a story or serve in the way of creating change in any way, shape, or form. Instead, static characters are usually minor characters. These characters still provide the author with the opportunity to use them as tools to spark change in the main characters, but they are not always required to change in order for the successful progression of the story.

Round Characters are unlike dynamic characters and unlike static characters altogether. These characters are ones that feature highly complex personalities. They may experience frequent conflicts, or they may even contradict themselves on a regular basis. These characters are also rarely used as major characters because the required personality type does not serve as a powerful foundation to generate a dynamic and moving character.

Flat Characters, unlike rounded characters, flat characters are typically notable for one single personality trait. This characteristic is one that should be the primary defining factor, influence, and expression that is used by the character. When you are creating a flat character, they are often much like a static character. And, similar to static characters, they are not suitable for the central characters because this personality does not provide the author with the opportunity to generate a moving enough character that will lead someone through a plot line.

Stock Characters are considered to be stereotypical characters that are almost expected in certain stories. For example, a cynical but moral private eye, mad scientists, and faithful sidekicks are all stock characters. These are all people that you would expect to be present in certain books. They generate the name "stock character" because of repetitive use in certain story types and structures. These characters typically have flat personalities, but may also have rounded personalities in some cases. They are a great element to add to your story because they give the reader something that they can identify with and expect, as well as someone that helps them feel like they can better relate to the story. It is a great way to give your reader a point to engage with through providing them with a familiar presence.

Protagonist is the word used to describe the central character in your story. This is the primary character that the story follows. They are at the center of your central characters, and they provide the main storyline. Most people call this the "main character," and they are identified as the "most important role in the story" to most, although this is not entirely true. Although this person is the reason the story exists, they are not the only one responsible for moving the plot forward. Therefore they are not the most important role. Still, they are highly important. This character should be dynamic and well-developed, as this will be the one your reader is going to follow most. Although the protagonist may not be the most likable character, they are the one that should be used in order to command that the reader experiences emotions, particularly empathy, for them. This way they can be used to draw the story forward and keep the reader engaged along the way.

Antagonist is the word used to describe either a character or a situation that operates against the protagonist. This is the opposition and the oppressive force that is trying to stop or otherwise hinder the success of the protagonist. This is the obstacle the protagonist faces that they must find the strength, knowledge, and power to overcome if they are going to generate a successful happy-ending story. As mentioned in the beginning, the antagonist can be a character *or* a situation. It can also be both. Even if you are using a situation instead of a character for your antagonistic force, you still want to go through the effort of making it well-developed so that the reader can believe it and understand why it is such a threat to the protagonist and their stakes.

Anti-Hero is a word used to describe a character that presents itself in certain stories. This is usually the protagonist, and they are called the anti-hero because they possess many features that make them unlikeable. They may have questionable morals, negative behavioral traits, or other characteristics that are not typically admired by the average person. This person may be the kind of individual that your reader would never want to associate with or root for, but still, they are the center of the story, and they find themselves following them and feeling empathy for this character when certain events happen. Writing an anti-hero protagonist can be difficult, but if you can master it, it is a great practice to help you increase your ability to generate empathy and emotional attachments between readers and your characters.

Foil Characters are those who have personalities and characteristics that often clash with other central characters in the novel. These characters may be used to represent the antagonist or a supporting character. They are designed by creating a character who has qualities that contrast the protagonist's character, or another important character within' the storyline. This contrast may seem unimportant, but from a writer's perspective, it provides you with the opportunity to highlight certain characteristics about your protagonist or other central character by emphasizing the differences between them and the foil character.

Symbolic Characters are ones that are used to resemble major parts of society through one character. These characters may be any major or minor character within' your story, so long as the entire purpose of the character is to highlight a certain aspect of society through their actions, beliefs, and values.

How Characters Are Presented and Revealed

Presenting and revealing characters is your opportunity to teach your reader who the character is and what they're all about. This is where you get the ability to introduce them to different characteristics and traits that the reader should know about the character, and how these traits contribute to the way that the character ties into the storyline.

There are only two ways that you can present your characters to your readers: either through direct or indirect presentation.

Direct presentation is the method you use when you are directly telling your readers about who the character is. For example, if you were to write "Presenting to you, Christopher Adams, a self-righteous, ignorant, and exploitative agent who preys on his clients for their money." In this circumstance, you are directly telling your reader who Christopher Adams is and what his most outstanding traits are. You can also do it in a more positive light, such as "Meet Mary Willows, a school teacher who spends her time eating peanut butter sandwiches and teaching preschoolers how to count to five. She is always bright and cheery, and will put a smile on your face faster than even a puppy could." In essence, direct presentation is described as any type of presentation you make whereby you tell the reader what they need to know.

Indirection Presentation is naturally the exact opposite of direct presentation. This is the tactic you use when you leave it up to the reader to get to know a character through his or her words, thoughts, and actions. They get to know this person through what they say and do throughout the book, allowing them to generate their own theories on who this character is. Still, you use their words and actions to help you create the overall illusion as to what makes the character who they are. This form of presentation is very similar to the natural way that we get to know people since we are not given direct answers when we meet people.

Instead, we have to learn about them based on what they say and do. Unlike direct presentation, indirect presentation is the tactic used when authors allow readers to formulate judgments and opinions on characters without ever telling them about the quality traits these characters have. Sometimes the reader will know exactly who the character is and their judgment is right, and other times they will be proven wrong over the course of the book.

To make it easier for you to use these two presentation methods to introduce who your characters are, we have compiled a list of the eleven basic ways that you can present your characters to your readers. This list is compiled to provide examples of both direct and indirect presentation methods. You can also use it as a test to see if you can determine which would be considered direct and which would be considered indirect so that you can better understand how both of these presentation styles work.

1. Present your character by having them say things in a particular way.

2. Present your character by having them say certain things.

3. Present your character by providing insight into their environment.

4. Present your character by exploring what they think.

5. Present your character by providing a physical description of them.

6. Present your character by providing a psychological description of them.

7. Present your character by telling readers what other people say or think about them.

8. Present your character by having them do certain things.

9. Present your character by having them do things in a particular way.

10. Present your character by the way that they react to other's actions and words.

11. Present your character by the way that they react to their own actions and words.

Chapter 2: What Makes a Character Great

Since you are researching how to make the characters for your novel, let's assume that you don't just want to make a good character. Instead, you want to make a great character. You want to make the kind of character that people are eager to read more about. This character is one that the reader can somehow attach to. It also gives you the best tool to help you move your story forward, regardless of what type of character you are creating. Some of these techniques should be used on all characters while others only need to be used on a few, which you will learn about as you read on. Still, every character in your novel is important to the storyline itself. Therefore, they all need to be great characters. This chapter will help you identify exactly what is required in order for you to be able to do just that.

Have Characters that Are Likeable

While not all of your characters have to be likable, many should be. Your protagonist, for example, should be a likable character unless you are spinning them off as an anti-hero. Having likable characters in your book will make people have an easier ability to emotionally connect to your characters. Just as you would prefer to spend time with and invest your energy in people you like in real life when people read they also like to invest their energy and attention into characters that they like. At least a few of your characters should be likable so that your reader feels as though they can relate to the character and generate some form of emotional attachment and relationship with that character as they read your story.

As you are creating likable characters, however, avoid making them saint-like. You do not want to have a character that is *too* likable or features little to no flaws because this actually goes back in the opposite direction. It takes away from the realistic values of your character and makes them seem unapproachable, which, ironically makes them unlikeable. So, avoid trying to make your characters *too* likable, or people won't like them! Instead, create a realistic character who has believable flaws that are enough to balance out their likable qualities so that they are still likeable while also being realistic and relatable.

Have Characters that Are Not Likeable

In addition to having characters that are likable, you need to have ones that aren't! Any real-life story would include people who are not liked by the protagonist, and who may be unlikeable in general. These are the ones whose flaws outweigh their good traits. They are still human, therefore they still naturally have some good qualities to them, but overall they are not likable as a person. In a typical story, this is your antagonist, but it doesn't always have to be. Furthermore, you can have more people who are unlikeable, such as someone who is related to or close to the protagonist. Using unlikeable characters helps to balance out the number of likable characters you have, thus making the story sound more relatable and realistic.

Again, you don't want to create a character that is *too* unlikeable, or people aren't going to believe it. Typically, even the worst people have some positive characteristics to them that make them worth having empathy for, even if we don't tend to like them in general. Make sure that you keep your unlikeable character's human by giving them some characteristics that make them seem as though they *could* be likable in some way or another, even if only a little.

Make Your Characters Good at What They Do

Even though your characters, particularly your protagonist, should face difficulties and come to the end of their rope once or twice before finally succeeding, they should still succeed in the end. Furthermore, they should be good at what they do, even if it isn't always enough to get them to a full success. For example, they should be a phenomenal secret agent that is exposed to acts of god that make it impossible for them to capture the bad guy until *finally* things go right and they succeed at last. Even if they make mistakes from time to time or they struggle to be the best here and there, they should typically be good at what they do. If they aren't, people are going to wonder why they are even trying to begin with and it will make the story unlikeable.

Think about stories such as the James Bond ones. If James Bond were to fail every mission he ever set out to accomplish it would not make for a good story. People may laugh their way through one show, but it would not last, and they certainly wouldn't have many different movies based on this hero. Likewise, your heroic character should be good at what they do, and they should be worthy of your reader cheering them on for the duration of your story.

Give Your Characters a Strong Charisma

Having characters that are charismatic increases their likeability. It doesn't only draw in other characters, but it draws in the reader as well. While charisma as far as good looks can be a beneficial factor, this is more about their qualities. Make them someone who lights up the room when they walk in it. Maybe they are particularly happy, or they always have a good joke to share. Or, maybe they are great at complimenting others and making them feel good about themselves. Whatever way you choose to build charisma in the character, make sure you take the time to actually establish it. Remember, you want likable characters and charisma is one great way to create a character that can be liked. The more drawn into the character your reader is, the more invested they will become in your story overall.

Have Dynamic Characters

Characters that love to take driven action and grow alongside your plot line are great when it comes to building a strong book. As you know, it is good to have your protagonist as a dynamic character. However, you should consider adding a few other dynamic characters as well. Having the antagonistic character, as well as supporters of both the protagonist and antagonist being designed to be dynamic characters means that you have plenty of opportunities to pursue action in your story. It also makes the story much more relatable and realistic.

When you are creating dynamic characters, know that not every character in the story needs to be dynamic. In fact, it is better to have a strong balance between dynamic and static characters. Remember, in real life, we have a little bit of everything. If you can look at your own life, there are likely people who have never changed or haven't been in your own life story enough for their change to be recognized, and then there are those who have grown drastically since you met them. Just like in real life, your book needs to have a healthy mixture of both as well. This will ensure that your reader feels as though your story is compelling and enjoyable.

Let Your Characters Suffer

Some of the novels are going to require your characters to suffer. Conflicts, complex issues, and various situations would lead to any normal person facing the experience of suffering in their own life. The same goes for your characters. If someone dies, let the character suffer. Allow them to feel the suffering. If they lose something, something doesn't go their way, or they are otherwise facing challenges, allow them to experience some suffering alongside those challenges. This makes them more believable and relatable. Furthermore, it draws your reader's emotions into the story even more. Letting your character suffer somewhat is a great way to build empathy from your reader to your character. Once your reader has empathy, they are much more likely to care about what's next for your character. They want to see the character do well and they are eager to see them win, so the reader roots even more for your character. You can build on this throughout the story by introducing a few different instances of suffering. Just, as with everything, make sure you don't go overboard and have too much suffering, or the book will be too depressing and unbelievable to read!

Know Your Character Intimately

It is important that you know your character intimately. Even more intimately than your readers ever will, even though they need to get to know them intimately as well. When you know your characters intimately, you can easily talk about them, share their story, and give insight into their inner world. This is because you would know how they would think, speak, act, and react in various situations. You also know their preferences, dislikes, likes, and other important characteristics about them.

Think about someone that you know well. You have likely known someone at one point or another in your life so well that you know exactly what they would do or say in most situations. This is how intimately you need to know your characters, as this is the intimacy that will allow you to write about them in any and every situation that will arise throughout your novel. You should know exactly how that person would respond to everything you throw their way so that you can create a realistic and believable character. This is what takes your character from a profile on paper to a real person in your fiction novel.

Chapter 3: Character Building Step-by-Step

Now that you are clear on why characters are important, the basics about characters, and what makes a character great instead of just good, you are ready to start actually building your characters. As you go through this chapter, keep what you have already learned in mind as it will help you stay focused and create successful characters along the way.

In this chapter, you are going to discover step-by-step guidance for picking whom you want to cast in your book, as well as how you can develop each character so that they serve your book in a powerful and profound way. Depending on what type of character you are working towards developing, you will discover a guide to help you develop that kind of character. This will ensure that each character is developed enough to be useful in your novel, but that you aren't wasting your time over-developing characters that do not require it, such as minor static characters.

Choosing Your Cast

Before you begin developing your characters you need to decide which characters you want to cast in your book. That is, you need to decide how many characters you are going to need to actually write the book. While you may find that some additional ones come up or you feel naturally called to pull in new characters along the way, you should start out with a pretty strong idea as to whom your central, minor, and other characters are going to be from the beginning. Anyone who is going to be essential to your central story should be outlined and developed before you begin writing. This will ensure that you know exactly how and when to present them, and their presentation is natural and strong based on their unique character and role in the novel.

The best way to choose how many characters you need for your novel is to refer back to your story structure and outline. Looking at your story structure and outline will give you the opportunity to consider each major plot point. As you do, consider which characters should be present for the plot point, as well as which ones are necessary for it. Take your time and work your way through the plot, picking out characters as you go. Once you have, take a look at the "in between" parts, too. For example, in between major plot points, you may need additional characters to keep the story flowing, such as people in line at a bank or the cashier at the local grocer. This is the best way to determine what characters you need in your novel and will have you well on your way to a strong character roster.

Once you have determined which characters are needed for the plot, you want to get more specific about them. First, make sure that you haven't picked too many characters. A book with too many characters can be overwhelming and can lead to your reader forgetting who is who. However, you want to make sure that you have enough that you can make it feel like real life. The best way to make sure you have enough characters, and not too few or too many, is to make sure that every single character you choose to create is essential to the story itself. Then, you need to decide what kind of character they're going to be. Are they going to be a major character or a minor character? Additionally, will they be round, flat, static, or dynamic? Pay attention to these features as they will help you determine how to create them.

Creating Your Characters

Central characters are the main characters in your novel. They include the protagonist, the antagonist, and any other characters that are regularly involved in the plot, including major plot scenes. When you are creating central characters, you want to go heavily into depth about who they are and why they are that way. Below you will find several categories filled with questions. Answering these questions will help you answer about who your character is, which will help you develop them and learn a great deal of information about them. This way you can get to know them intimately and write about them effortlessly.

Character's General Information

1. What is your character's name?

2. Do they have a nickname? If so, what is the story behind it and who gave it to them?

3. Do they like their nickname?

4. What is their birthday?

5. Where were they born?

6. What ethnicity are they?

7. Do they have any religious views?

8. Do they practice their religion?

9. Where do they currently live? (Be specific with their address)

10. Do they rent the place or own it?

11. Briefly describe their home.

12. Does anyone else live with them?

13. What is it like where they live? (i.e., city, town, etc.)

14. Do they like living here? If not, why not? Where would they rather be?

15. What type of home décor do they have? (i.e., expensive, neat, inexpensive, comfortable, etc.)

16. What is the first impression someone would have to their home?

17. Do they have pets? If not, why not? If they do, what kind, what are their names, and how many? How do they treat their pets?

18. What job do they presently have, how long have they had it for, and where is their job located?

19. Do they like their job?

20. How much money do they make?

21. What educational background do they have?

22. Do they drive? If so, what kind of vehicle do they have? Be specific.

23. What is their sexuality?

24. Are they in a romantic relationship with anyone? If so, who and for how long?

25. Do they have any previous romantic partners that are significant to the story?

26. What do they call their current spouse? (i.e., nicknames)

27. How did they meet their spouse?

28. Do they have any children? Give specific details if they do. (i.e., age, birthday, gender, name, who the parents are, etc.)

29. If they have children, describe the relationship they share with each child.

Physical Appearance

1. How tall is this character?

2. What do they weigh?

3. What body type do they have? (i.e., skinny, curvy, overweight, athletic, etc.)

4. What color are their eyes?

5. Do they use glasses, contacts, or hearing aids? Or any other medical devices?

6. What is their skin tone?

7. Do they have any prominent features that one might notice about them? (i.e., freckles, birthmark, scar, tattoos, etc.)

8. What is their face shape?

9. Whom do they look similar to?

10. What is their overall health like?

11. Do they have any chronic illnesses or conditions?

12. Are there any current health problems they are facing?

13. How do they dress? (Including cost range of clothes and specific style)

14. Do they dress to be noticed, or just to be dressed?

15. Do they wear any special or significant pieces of jewelry or accessories?

16. How does this character approach their grooming habits? (i.e., extremely neat, unkempt, etc.) Why do they groom themselves this way?

17. What hairstyle does this character have?

18. What is the natural hair texture for this character?

19. If they typically groom their hair for a different texture, what is it?

20. What is their natural hair color?

21. If they dye their hair, what color is it now?

Communication

1. When communicating, what is the pace that this person communicates with? (i.e., fast, slow, average)

2. What tone of voice do they have?

3. Do they have any words they tend to use or favor in general conversation?

4. What are their vocabulary patterns? (I.e., educated, precise, vulgar, etc.)

5. What is their demeanor when communicating? (I.e., cool and confident, nervous, etc.)

6. What posture do they tend to have?

7. Do they use gestures frequently in communication? If so, how often?

8. What are their common body language gestures or signals? (i.e., nail-biting, clenching fists, shoving hands in pockets, etc.)

Daily Behaviors & Habits

1. How does this character manage their finances? (i.e., saves a lot, living paycheck to paycheck, etc.)

2. Do they acquire any of their finances illegally? If so, how?

3. Do they have any personal habits that may be based on addictions? (i.e., drinking, smoking, gambling, etc.)

4. What is their morning routine? Be specific.

5. What does their average day look like? Be specific.

6. Do they ever have lunch in any particular spot?

7. What is your character's dinner routine? Be specific.

8. What does your character do after dinner? Be specific.

9. What is your character's bedtime routine? Be specific.

10. Does your character have any skills or talents? If so, do they share them or are they hidden and/or kept private?

11. What is your character unskilled at, or bad at? How do they feel about these flaws?

12. Do they have any hobbies?

Character's Past

1. Where is your character's hometown?

2. What was their childhood like? Do they remember it?

3. What is their earliest memory?

4. What is their saddest memory?

5. What is their happiest memory?

6. Did your character attend school? If so, how much? Did they enjoy school? Why or why not?

7. What is the most significant event that took place in your character's childhood?

8. Do they have any other significant childhood events?

9. What past jobs have they had that are significant to them?

10. Do they have a criminal record?

11. If your character does have a criminal record, how did they get it and where were they when the event happened?

12. Did they get any convictions or sentences? Did they serve time?

13. Who was the first person that your character loved?

14. When was their first sexual experience? Do think look back on it as a positive memory or a negative one?

15. Has your character experienced any major accidents or traumas in their life? If so, are they still affected by them? How?

Family Tree

1. Who is your character's mother? What is her full name?

2. Is she alive or deceased?

3. What is or was the mother's occupation?

4. What is the relationship that your character shares with their mother?

5. Who is your character's father? What is his full name?

6. Is he alive or deceased?

7. What is or was the father's occupation?

8. What is the relationship that your character shares with their father?

9. Does the character have any additional parental figures, such as a step-parent, foster parents, adoptive parents, biological parents, or even an adult who was of parental influence in their life such as a close family friend?

10. If they were adopted, do they know about it?

11. Does your character have any siblings? If so, list them by age in birth order. Include their names and how they are related to the character. (i.e., full sibling, step-sibling, half-sibling, etc.)

12. What type of relationship does your character share with each of their siblings?

13. Does your character have any nieces or nephews? If so, what are the relationship(s) like?

14. Do they have any in-laws? If so, what are the relationship(s) like?

15. Who else is a part of the character's family that is significant to the story, aside from those already listed?

Relationships

1. Who is your character's best or closest friend? How long have they known each other and where did they meet?

2. Do they have any other close friends? If so, how long has your character known them and where did they meet?

3. How is your character perceived by their friends?

4. How is your character perceived by strangers?

5. How is your character perceived by their spouse or lover?

6. How is your character perceived by their past spouses/lovers?

7. How is your character perceived by their children, if they have any?

8. How is your character perceived by their other family members?

9. How is your character perceived by the opposite sex?

10. How is your character perceived by children in general?

11. How is your character perceived by others who have more success than them?

12. How is your character perceived by others who have less success than them?

13. How is your character perceived by their boss, if they have one?

14. How is your character perceived by their co-workers?

15. How is your character perceived by their competitors?

16. How is your character perceived by authorities? (i.e., police, doctors, attorneys, etc.)

17. How does your character react to people who challenge them?

18. How does your character react to people who anger them?

19. How does your character react to people who ask for help?

20. What do others tend to like most about your character?

21. What do they like least or consider to be the character's biggest flaw?

22. Does this character have any secret attractions to others? If so, have they been explored?

23. In romantic relationships, is your character typically faithful or unfaithful? If they are unfaithful, does their partner(s) know it?

24. What are they like during sexual encounters? (inhibited and shy or outgoing and wild?) Does this change over the course of the story or their life? If it does, why?

25. Who does your character like the least out of everyone in the story? Why?

26. Who does your character like the most out of everyone in the story? Why?

27. Who does your character consider to be the most important person in their life right now, and why do they feel this way?

28. Who is your character romantically attracted to at the moment, and why?

29. Who is your character's role model or idol? Why? And are they famous, or no?

30. Who does your character consider to be their enemy, if anyone?

31. Who does your character tend to misjudge or misunderstand the most?

32. Who tends to misunderstand or misjudge your character the most?

33. Is there anyone whom your character has lost touch within their lifetime who was significant to them? If so, why and how has it affected your character?

34. What was the worst ending to any relationship your character has had? (romantic or otherwise)

35. Who do they typically rely on when it comes to receiving advice?

36. Who does your character tend to rely on when it comes to emotional support?

37. Who does your character support, either emotionally or with advice, the most?

Attitude & Beliefs

1. Does your character have any psychological issues such as phobias, mental illnesses, or otherwise?

2. Do they tend to be optimistic or pessimistic?

3. Do you know the Meyer Briggs personality type for your character? (This can give a lot of information about how they would react and respond in a variety of situations.)

4. When is your character the most comfortable in life? (i.e., when drinking, when with certain people, when alone, etc.)

5. When are they the least comfortable? (i.e., when public speaking, in certain locations, around certain people, when drinking, etc.)

6. Does your character tend to be cautious, reckless, or brave in how they approach their life?

7. What does your character value and prioritize the most? (i.e., family, religion, friends, fun, money, success, etc.)

8. Who does your character love the best?

9. What or who would your character be willing to die for?

10. How does your character tend to be towards others? (i.e., compassionate, arrogant, selfish, sensitive, etc.)

11. What is the personal philosophy of your character?

12. What is your character most embarrassed about?

13. What is their greatest wish?

14. Do they have any prejudices against other people? If so, what and why?

15. What are their political beliefs?

16. Do they believe in any superstitions, fate, or destiny?

17. What is the greatest strength that your character possesses?

18. What is the greatest weakness that your character possesses?

19. What other positive or strong characteristics does your character possess?

20. What other negative or weak characteristics does your character possess?

21. What does your character favor most about their own attributes? (Both physical and personality-wise)

22. What does your character despise most about their own attributes? (Both physical and personality-wise)

23. Are these feelings accurate, or are they over or underplayed?

24. How does your character think other people perceive them? Is this accurate?

25. What does your character regret the most in life?

26. Do they have any other regrets?

27. What are the biggest secrets that your character has?

28. Does anyone else know about these secrets? If so, who?

29. How do they react in a crisis?

30. What tends to cause the most problems in their life? (i.e., finances, colleagues, friends, family, health, etc.)

31. How do they react to change?

32. Do they have any quirks?

33. What would your character like to change about themselves the most?

34. Give a short paragraph (100 words or less) of the character describing themselves to others.

35. What are their short-term goals?

36. What are their long-term goals?

37. Do they have any plans to achieve the goals, or do they believe they are out of reach?

38. How would others be affected by your character reaching these goals? Do this effects matter to your character?

39. If anything is stopping your character from achieving their goals, what is it?

40. What are they actively working to protect, keep, or gain right now?

41. What event or situation do they most fear or dread being in?

42. What person would your character want to be, if they could be anyone?

43. Who would they absolutely not want to be?

Likes & Favorites

1. What is your character's favorite food?

2. What is your character's favorite drink?

3. What color do they like most?

4. Do they have a favorite book?

5. Do they have a favorite film?

6. What song or music genre do they prefer?

7. Do they watch TV? If so, what do they watch?

8. Does your character have a favorite sport?

9. Does your character have a motto or a quote that they like?

10. Where do they like to hang out or spend most of their time?

11. What do they own that is their favorite possession?

This list may seem extremely exhausting, but trust that all of this information will help you get to know your character intimately. Once you have the answers to all of these questions, you will know your character so well that it will be effortless for you to write about them and their natural evolution over the course of your novel. Do your best to fill in the entire questionnaire so that you have plenty of material to write on and that nothing is left up to chance. A writer who has extremely strong characters is one who knows their characters so well that they could easily answer any of these questions about them. Keep your character profile handy so that you can refer back to it during the writing process as needed.

A Word on Minor Characters

Naturally, you don't need to have an elaborate profile for your minor characters. Instead, go through the list and pick the questions that you feel relate most to how the character fits into the story. For example, if it is a friend from high school that your protagonist sees once or twice during the entire book, you likely don't need to include much. You may want to fill out the general section, the past section, and the likes and favorites section. Even then, it may not be necessary for you to fill out the entire thing. When it comes to designing minor characters, use your judgment to create a character that has depth, without wasting your time developing a character further than you actually need to for the benefit of your overall book.

Chapter 4: Creating Expression

How your character expresses themselves is a really important part of how they contribute to the story itself. Their expression is ultimately how your character conveys themselves to others. This will be how they express their thoughts and opinions, and how they portray themselves to others to interpret them and who they are. You want to make sure that, just like with your character development, you develop how your character expresses themselves as well. While this part of the book will not go into as elaborate of a guide as the previous chapter did, we will explore various ways that you can create an expression for your character, as well as for all of the characters within' your book as a whole.

Catch Phrases

Having characters have their own catchphrases is a great way to build an expression in your character and give them a unique voice. This should be a catchphrase that only one character uses, even though other characters may sometimes paraphrase that character to be funny or to otherwise quote them. Still, it should be known that this phrase is unique to that specific character.

Don't overuse catch phrases in your book or it will take away from the value of them. Ideally, only one or *maybe* two characters should have a catch phrase in your book. Also, avoid it being the main character unless they are only going to use the catchphrase from time to time. The catch phrase is a great way to give foreshadowing effects, but with too many, it can take away and just sound cheesy or poorly written.

Group-Specific Slang Words

If you look at most friend groups in real life, they have their own way of speaking. This way of speaking often includes their own selection of slang words. If you want to increase the expression and voice of your overall group, as well as each character that is a part of it, seek to make slang words or group mottos that are used by everyone in the group. However, make sure that none of the slang or mottos are anywhere close to the one character's catchphrase or you will confuse the reader. Instead, simply choose expressions and terms that this group will speak in that others likely don't. This makes them unique and gives them a very realistic feel, since this is completely natural behavior in real life, too.

Other Worldly Slang

If you are writing a fantasy book that takes your characters to another world, consider using other worldly slang that you have made up in order to help set them apart. In a group, each person speaks differently from one another, just as how each individual in a country – or likely the entire world – speaks differently. You likely wouldn't go to a different planet and hear everyone speaking in typical American dialect. For that reason, it is a good idea to create and include other worldly phrases and slang that help the reader differentiate the characters.

Gender-Specific Phrases

If you ever pay attention to a real-life crowd, men and women tend to express themselves in extremely different ways. You can bring this type of gender-specific expression into your novel, too. And, in fact, you should. By including as many different unique elements of expression in your novel as you can, you make the novel more believable, and your readers have an easier time relating to it. While you don't have to use gender stereotypes to create the expressions between each gender, you should make it clear that they are two different genders speaking and expressing themselves. If you need inspiration, spend some time with a group of males and then spend some time with a group of females and you will see the differences. If you want to take it even further, afterward spend some time with a mixed group and you will still notice that each gender expresses themselves differently, even in front of the other sex.

Career and Industry Jargon

People in different careers and industries typically speak in unique tongues. They have industry and career-specific jargon that they use when they are talking to their colleagues. When you are building characters who have jobs, careers, or are heavily involved in certain industries, make sure that you include some jargon from that job, career, or industry in their vocabulary. In the real world, people would naturally pick up on and use this jargon. Therefore, your character should too.

Body Language

It is no secret that body language is a major part of how we communicate with others and express ourselves. Use body language in your book, too. If characters are feeling attacked or bullied and they are feeling particularly low or closed off, have them standing with a closed expression such as with their arms crossed and skulking away from the attacker. If the character is happy, have them standing tall and proud with their body casual but a bright smile on their face. Using body language as a means to help your characters communicate on an even more advanced level will help you when it comes to expressing your characters. While you don't need to explain their body language at every moment, a good idea is to introduce what they look like when they're feeling neutral and then only talk about their body language if it is vastly different from what it would be when they're in that neutral state. If you are unsure about what body language people would be using when they're talking or when they're feeling different things, consider briefly studying it. There are many online and print resources available that are made specifically to help people further understand body language. Knowing it more intimately may help you when it comes to helping your character express themselves.

Sometimes when you are creating certain scenes, body language can speak more to the reader and other characters than the communicating character's own words will. For example, if the character is lying to someone else, have their words telling a lie while their body exposes the truth about them lying. Maybe they are telling a lie, and in the meantime, they are sweating, and they have shoved their hands into their pockets. Body language can teach people a lot about what is truly going on in your character's mind, beyond what they say, so be sure to use it at the appropriate times for greater expression.

Dialect

Make sure your character's dialect is true to where they come from. If they are from the southern states, for example, have them use a southern dialect. You may even have presented their accent to the reader. If they are from somewhere else, such as a foreign country, use the dialect that is natural to where that person comes from. Using proper native dialect not only helps create a realistic element to your characters but it also helps you contrast between your characters if you have a few that are from different areas or countries.

Regional Slang

Most regions have their own slang that is unique from other regions. Just like their dialect differs from place to place, so too does their choice in slang words. In the majority of cases kids and teens are more likely to use slang over adults, so make sure that the younger demographic uses a lot more slang than the older demographic. Furthermore, ensure that the slang that your younger demographic is using is age specific and that your older demographic is using age-specific terms. The adults may occasionally use terms from the younger demographic, but don't make this happen often and make sure that you make it clear that they have borrowed it from someone in the younger generation.

General Vocabulary

In addition to all of the other steps in this chapter, make sure that you take a look at your character's vocabulary in general. Everyone tends to speak a certain way, often slightly different from other people. To put it bluntly, there are some people that just don't say some things because it's not a part of their standard vocabulary. The best thing to do is to get an idea of what your character's overall vocabulary is. Since vocabulary and the words, they could use go so far, the better idea is to outline what they don't say and would never say. This helps you get an idea for their style of communication and what they actually would say.

Creating expression takes time and practice, but if you follow these tips and have patience, you should be well on your way to creating strong terms of expression for all of your characters. Remember, when it comes to really planning out each character, don't worry too much about creating a very specific set of expressions for characters who have an extremely minor role in the story. Instead, focus on those who are minor but recurring, or those who are central characters. These are the ones who you really want to go into depth with when planning their expressions. Take your time and work through each of these steps while planning out how the character will express themselves in each one and use this as your opportunity to get to know your character even more. This will make it much simpler to know how your character will express themselves and communicate with others in your novel.

Chapter 5: Bringing Your Character to Life

Finally, you want to bring your character to life! This is the part of the process where you take that perfect profile you've made on paper, and you start bringing each character to life for the first time. This is where you get to turn them into real characters that will have prominent roles in your novel in one way or another. Through the following steps, you will tie up any loose ends and then ultimately unleash your character into the world. Once this part of the process is done, you can start writing your story, trusting that your characters will be strong enough to support the plot line and make your story truly great.

Use Inspiration from People You Actually Know

There is a good chance that the characters you have made somehow resemble someone you already know in real life. When we are creating characters, we are often drawn on inspiration from those that we already know. Don't feel shy when doing this! When you are writing, feel open to the idea of drawing on more inspiration for situations where you might need it. For example, if you are truly struggling to identify how your character would act, react, respond, or speak in any given situation, draw inspiration from that person! This will help their actions flow naturally so that they seem realistic to who the character truly is. It is never a bad thing to draw on this inspiration, so keep it handy and use it at your own discretion to help increase the quality of your story, simplify the writing process, and create a compelling character that fits perfectly into your story.

Play on the Element of Surprise

Sometimes readers expect a certain thing when they are reading. For example, if your characters are going into a night club your reader will likely expect that the bouncer is some big gangly guy who would easily knock anyone down who tried to slip through uninvited. Instead of simply going with the person that your reader would assume the character would look like, pick someone unique who makes your reader feel surprised towards who is playing the role. For example, you might pick a slender and somewhat lanky character who looks like they would struggle to keep a small dog back, let alone a potential customer who was serious about getting in. Instead of having a tall, white, male lawyer, consider having someone from a completely different demographic. Character's don't need to be exactly who you would assume they would be. In fact, they're often better when they aren't whom you expect them to be, yet this is still phenomenal at their role.

In addition to using the element of surprise in your characters, use it in your events, too. Don't be afraid to make the unexpected happen and keep your readers on their toes. Use events that they wouldn't have expected create settings that are unlike what they would have expected, and ultimately give your reader a reason to think "Oh, wow! Really?" This element of surprise is a great way to bring your characters and book itself to life. Most real-life experiences don't go as planned and often many unexpected events, people, and circumstances come to light in our lives. Do the same with your book, both with characters, events, and circumstances. You want your reader to feel like it is real life and that they never know what to expect from one day to another. This increases the value of your story and also heightens your reader's engagement and commitment towards your book.

Use Contradictions

Strong characters often have qualities that are highly contradictory. People aren't always as they seem, and so your character's shouldn't be as well. A great way to increase the livelihood of your characters and bring them to life is to give them contradictions. For example, an incredibly sporty race car driver who is obsessed with the opera. Using these contradictions in your characters remind people that they're human and that they aren't always logical box-fitting characters. Instead, they are real, and they have interesting quirks about them just like we all do.

Give Your Characters Goals

In the character developing chapter we explored the goals that your character has, but now we really want to emphasize on that. Giving your character's goals, hopes, dreams, and fantasies about how they want the future to be for themselves make them a lot more life-like. Real life people always have some form of goal or dream, whether they talk about it or not. Giving your characters these features is important because it gives them something to look forward to, and something for your reader to look forward to with them. It gives your reader a deeper insight into your character's inner world and what makes them tick, therefore making your reader feel a lot more connected to your character.

Discover Their Image

Through the character development process, we discovered many identifying factors that shed light on what your character's actual image was, but if you really want to make them life-like, you want to discover exactly what it is like. One great way to do this is to find a picture of someone on Google or otherwise who represents your character. They should look similar both in physical appearances and in the way they present themselves through style and expression. Many great writers claim that they will even print these pictures off and keep them nearby so that they can truly look at their characters and gain insight from them during the writing process, to help progress the story along. If this feels right for you, certainly go ahead and borrow this tip from other writers.

One thing to note about your character's image is that despite you know it intimately, you don't want to over explain it to your readers. Instead, give away important pieces of information but let your reader develop a picture in their own mind. When your reader generates their own image of who your character is and what they look like it becomes more engaging and more personal. Then, your reader is more likely to connect with your character and feel a form of emotional attachment towards them.

Listen to Them

Many writers claim that they can actually *hear* their character's voices. They start often by hearing a voice on the television or somewhere in public that sounds extremely similar to their character's own voice. Then, they listen to that person and try to generate a total voice from it. Through that, they are able to listen to the voice of the character and use that to help them move forward.

Each character has their own unique voice. This is a combination of how they speak, what they are saying, and all of the tone and emotion that goes into their words. You want to discover the voice of each of your characters when you are writing because this makes the sense of expression and speaking for them much easier. This is where you get the opportunity to bring them to life because they become a voice that, eventually, everybody hears somewhere. They may also hear it through someone on television or in public, but ultimately they can relate it back and go "hey that sounds like so and so from that book I just read!" When this happens, you have truly made your character life-like to the highest degree.

Practice

It may take some time, but as with all things, you need to practice. Practicing bringing your characters to life and making them realistic is a great way to truly discover how you can do it to the highest of your abilities. At first, it may feel uncomfortable or even unnatural, but quickly you will find an opportunity to make your characters even more life-like, and it will all just flow together.

One great way to practice is to consider an everyday situation. It doesn't have to be one that is going to be involved in your book, just consider an everyday situation, such as going into a coffee shop and talking to the barista. Then, write a few paragraphs for each character that you are trying to bring to life. Consider how they would walk into the café, how they would communicate with the barista, where they would go to stand after they've ordered, how they would carry their coffees, whether they would drink the coffee there or go elsewhere. Consider whether they have someone with them or if they're alone. How do they express themselves to other patrons in the coffee shop? Get very specific about how their visit would go through these paragraphs. This is a great way to really consider how your character would react in everyday situations, thus making it a lot easier for you to get to know your own character personally. Remember, once you know them intimately it becomes a lot easier to share them with your readers.

Give Your Characters Plenty of Opportunities to Show Up

Giving your character the opportunity to show the reader how they react in different situations is a great way to bring them to life. Put your characters into many different situations and give your reader the opportunity to see them in action in every single one. Share about how your character acts in these situations, what they are thinking, and what they say. Let your reader have an idea of what your character's intentions are and perhaps even what got them into this situation in the first place.

Giving your character plenty of chances to show up and experience many different situations that they can take action in gives you the opportunity to highlight them from different angles. You can show your reader what that character is like when they're angry, sad, happy, disappointed, unimpressed, hurt, and virtually any other emotion. When you explore your character under these different lights through naturally unfolding events, you make it a lot easier for you to give your reader a more intimate view of your character, too.

Successful stories are those that bring characters to life and make readers believe that they are real people. If you think back to any fiction novel you have read in the past, you can likely conclude that the best ones were the ones where you grieved the end of the book because it felt like you had truly lost someone from your life. *That's* how good your characters can become when you follow these guides and effectively bring them to life for your readers. And, although it may seem difficult, it truly isn't. Follow these steps, and you will have a life-like character playing on the heartstrings of your own readers in no time.

Conclusion

Thank you for reading *"Character Development: Step-by-Step | Essential Story Character Creation, Character Expression and Character Building Tricks Any Writer Can Learn"*.

I hope that you were able to learn plenty of information about how you can create a phenomenal character for your own novel throughout this book. By using the in-depth character creation guide, following the tips on how to build your character, how to make them great, and how to bring them to life, you should have all of the tools you need to make a phenomenal character that will truly draw your readers in and help them generate a sense of emotional attachment to your characters.

The next step is to begin building your characters. If you haven't already, take the time to generate a profile for each of your central characters and all of your biggest minor characters. As well, create modified profiles for your minor characters. Remember that they don't need to be nearly as in-depth, but they do still need to be descriptive enough that you can create a truly strong character. Furthermore, make sure that you pay attention to the tips about how you can make a good character great, and about how you can then bring your characters to life. Ideally, your characters should be brought to life and made so great that your readers feel as though they are friends with that character. They may even grieve the loss of the character when the book ends, and there is nothing left for them to read. Using these tools and tricks, you can certainly create characters that good for your own novel.

Thank you, and best of luck! Have fun writing!

More by Sandy Marsh

Discover all books from the Writing Best Seller Series by Sandy Marsh at:

bit.ly/sandy-marsh

Book 1: *How to Write a Novel*

Book 2: *Outlining*

Book 3: *Story Structure*

Book 4: *Plotting*

Book 5: *Character Development*

Book 6: *How to Write a Screenplay*

Themed book bundles available at discounted prices:

bit.ly/sandy-marsh